BOA
EDITIONS
LIMITED

Before and After the Fall

Özvegy nők táncoltak

Micsoda korszak volt ez a miénk!
Micsoda század! Özvegy nők
táncoltak egymással a bálban
szomorún mosolyogva, harsány zenére.
Lappadt voltak, akár a teli sótök,
és rövidek, akár a dagasztott kenyér.
Néha meg-megbillent mögöttük
    az üstdob réztányérja,
        mint a teli Hold,
mikor katonatemetők fölé csusszan.
A teremben már sem jajveszékelt senki,
        Csak a villany aludt el többször.
Jártak az özvegyek így is,
        jártak sötétben,
            jártak elvásott szandáljukban
                és cipőjükben
nyögött alattuk az olajos padló ráncratlan,
nyögött, mintha garas árokban
egy haska lőtt férfi nyögne.

Before and After the Fall

New Poems by

Sándor Csoóri

Translated from the Hungarian by
Len Roberts

BOA Editions, Ltd. ❧ Rochester, NY ❧ 2004

Manufactured in the United States of America

First Edition
04 05 06 07 7 6 5 4 3 2 1

Publications by BOA Editions, Ltd.—
a not-for-profit corporation under section 501 (c) (3)
of the United States Internal Revenue Code—
are made possible with the assistance of grants from
the Literature Program of the New York State Council on the Arts,
the Literature Program of the National Endowment for the Arts,
the Sonia Raiziss Giop Charitable Foundation,
the Lannan Foundation,
as well as from the Mary S. Mulligan Charitable Trust,
the County of Monroe, NY,
the Rochester Area Community Foundation,
The CIRE Foundation,
and the Ames-Amzalak Memorial Trust.

Cover Design: Ben Peterson
Cover Art: "Untitled" by Stephen Carpenter, courtesy of the artist
Interior Design and Composition: Richard Foerster
Manufacturing: McNaughton & Gunn, Lithographers
BOA Logo: Mirko

LIBRARY OF CONGRESS CATALOGING-IN-PUBLICATION DATA

Csoóri, Sándor.
 [Poems. English. Selections]
 Before and after the fall : new poems / by Sándor Csoóri ; [translated by
Len Roberts]— 1st ed.
   p. cm. — (Lannan translations selection series)
 ISBN 1–929918–46–1 (pbk. : alk. paper) — ISBN 1–929918–47–X (hardcover :
alk. paper)
 I. Roberts, Len, 1947– II. Title. III. Series.

PH3213.C8145A56 2004
894'.51113—dc22

                                                              2004004651

NATIONAL
ENDOWMENT
FOR THE ARTS

State of the Arts

NYSCA

BOA Editions, Ltd.
Thom Ward, Editor
David Oliveiri, Chair
A. Poulin, Jr., President & Founder (1938–1996)
260 East Avenue, Rochester, NY 14604
www.boaeditions.org

CONTENTS

~~~

Part Two
After the Fall
Poems from *With Swans, in Cannon Fire* (1994)

INTRODUCTION

A leading contemporary Hungarian poet, essayist and scriptwriter, Sándor Csoóri has been called by Hungarian critics and poets, "the genius of discontent," "the greatest writer in Hungarian intellectual life," and "the gray eminence of the Good Cause." He has also been praised as the "national poet," one who has assumed the responsibility of his nation's physical and spiritual well-being. Csoóri's identification of his own fate with his country's places him in Fate-literature, the mainstream Hungarian literary tradition. In this tradition, the poet is the conscience and teacher of his country, verbalizing the problems of the Hungarian people and of humankind.

As witnessed in the two books gathered in this collection, *Monuments of the World* (1989), and *With Swans, in Cannon Fire* (1994), this duty entails the poetic recording of what Csoóri has termed "the chronic memory of violence." Csoóri speaks to his generation's hardships and struggles during World War II and the ensuing forty-five-year Communist rule, as well as to their accompanying sense of guilt and loss.

As forthright and outspoken after the Communists' fall in 1989 as he was before it, Csoóri displays a healthy skepticism about his newly liberated country's political and social agendas, going so far as to call himself the master of "fouled hope." Presented side-by-side, these two books present a major Eastern European poet's sometimes startling perspectives on pre- and post-Communist Hungary.

The Bird Takes Wing (1954), Csoóri's first collection, contains poetry that is direct, lyrical description, following the model of Sándor Petőfi, the great Hungarian poet-warrior of the nineteenth century. However, beginning with his next book, *Devil-Butterfly* (1957), Csoóri's poems begin to develop as Fate-literature. Here the poet assumes a more direct responsibility for (and makes more direct statements about) the plight of his country. It is not until his third book, though, *Escape from Loneliness* (1962), that he writes with the force and style characteristic of his poetry ever since. During this time Csoóri read and was greatly influenced by other European poets—Federico García Lorca, Paul Éluard, and Pierre Reverdy. These influences, coupled with his great interest in national folk tales and their tremendous emphasis upon the image, created the more symbolic and visionary voice that characterizes all of Csoóri's later poetry.

Csoóri was born in 1930 to a peasant family in Zámoly, Hungary. Returning to his village as a fifteen-year-old in 1945, after the village had changed hands seventeen times between the Germans and Russians, he faced the grim task of burying people and animals. Such memories, colored by a haunting sense of survivor's guilt, are presented in strikingly vivid images. His poetry becomes, then, an offering to the dead, an expiation of sorts, and, as he says, attempts at "failed resurrection." He cannot, as his speaker complains in "I, Too, Might Have Been," "stop dreaming about rooms grown sooty, / and fluttering bloody swans caught in cannon fire."

"Returning Home from Flight after the War" captures one of his earliest such memories of his ravaged homeland:

> I came home and the house was gone. . . .
> What mines, shells
>   and armies danced here?
> What fists? The milking stool,
> like a suckling, lay on its back
> with dead, twisted legs.
> Not a tablespoon in the dust,
> not a knife, not a living plate,
> not a cloud snagged on a pear bough.

In addition to faithfully recording these varied nightmares of the war, Csoóri has been concerned with the great sense of personal and public betrayal he and members of his generation felt during the Communist rule of Hungary from 1945 to 1989. Insisting it is the individual's responsibility to retain integrity in the face of the depersonalizing modernist and socialist society—and the consequent idea that an individual who does not retain such integrity has betrayed both himself and his country—Csoóri returns again and again to this sense of betrayal and guilt in *Monuments of the World.* In "The Day After Easter," for example, the speaker directly claims his (and his generation's) culpability for living "behind doors and walls":

> The rooster crows the day after Easter, too,
>   though you've already guessed:
>   we are past every betrayal,
> past our years of Peter and Judas.
>
> We just stand here in the April garden . . .

and without words we forgive each other
 that we have lived behind doors and walls, in cellars
  studded with nails, cowardly,
in our poor, weapon-playing century

and that we have allowed lies to enter even the poems. . . .

The speaker in these poems also suffers what is commonly known as survivor's guilt for those who died. Such ghosts in Csoóri's past become mythical presentations of unending, nightmarish human violence and resulting guilt. In "May the Water Keep Vigil with Me," the speaker begins with a memory from the war, but quickly turns to addressing the "you, the long-banished," ending the poem with the public reference to his "European nightmare":

My head's heavy with drinking,
heavy with myself. In my recent dream
shirtless soldiers were running
and combing the ruffled park
with raised pitchforks.

Were they looking for me? For you, the long-banished?
I can't remember anymore. A blood stain
shone darkly on a stone. Past that, a storm lantern,
overturned. The flame mingled with the mud
and made everything so finite, so shameless.

I'd like to sleep for spite, too. I'd like to forget
my European nightmare, the horror of those flat on their backs. . . .

Csoóri is continually searching for answers (thus his persistent use of questions in the poems) to the existential problems he and his countrymen confront. But his poetry does not usually provide answers. It presents, dramatically, the dilemmas found. His speaker is typically alone, remembering a past that once held meaning, considering a future which, at best, will be filled with struggle and more death. The present, under Csoóri's unrelentingly honest gaze, is often one of lies and hypocrisy.

The second volume in this book, *With Swans, in Cannon Fire*, presents poems written from 1989 to 1994, several of which are much more openly critical of atrocities committed during the Communist era. "Wandering in a Former Party Office Building," for example, is an explicit attack against such atrocities, and could not have been published before 1989 without dire results. (Csoóri has experienced the power of the Party several times right from the start of his career. As early as 1965, for instance, he had a grant revoked, and was banned for a year from publication and public appearances.) The poem uses adamantly direct, strong images to place the reader at the scene of the crime:

> But in the nooks, here and there, hands ripped
> from wrists seem to appear, dusty interrogation lamps
> and faint blood on the floor. I don't understand:
> how could blood get here? How could scrotums
> tied off with string get here?

Although the speaker can address such atrocities more directly in these latter poems, he ironically still sees "new torturers" wherever he looks. For example, in "In Filtered Shade," the speaker describes what seems to be the new ruling class of Hungary: ". . . those well-groomed beer drinkers" who wear "on their necks, thick, hammered gold necklaces." The poem ends in a cynical stance: "Who can say it's not the hearts/of my new torturers growing stronger in them?"

In another poem written after the fall, "Sunday Still Life—with Table, with Knife," Csoóri again suggests that the new era has its very real fears and dangers, as did the old era:

> What could happen today
> has happened to us before:
> instead of tanks, loud circus vans
> tore up and down the cities' streets
> for weeks, stopping only now and then
> outside the morgues
> so we would not forget our fear.

Csoóri has made a point never to be hopeful because, as he has said, ". . . hopelessness: is self defense, the source of final calmness." His is an understandable, existential response to the repressive era that existed in Hungary for forty-five years after the war. It is startling, however, to discover how often in these poems written after the fall that the speaker questions his (and his country's) plight in the new era. "Is Anything Left?" presents a speaker who argues "it was better for me to be / hopeless but strong in the forty-year camp / than to be the master now of fouled hope."

A sense of estrangement and cynicism pervades several of these poems. Csoóri sees himself and his generation as "the truly laughable one-time winners—in defeat. . . ."

Such cynicism also drives "In Filtered Shade" where the speaker compares what seems to be Hungary's new ruling class, the "well-groomed beer drinkers," to

> . . . little Columbuses
> who have each just recently
> discovered
> a land swimming in haze
> with banana plantations,
> with green apples,
> with ant farms,
> and they already ship
> barrels of formic acid
> to armies secretly arming themselves.
> Or they trade women at bargain rates
> for classical ruins.

Csoóri's growing isolation becomes painfully clear—given his dutiful dedication to his country—in several of these latter poems. As the speaker in "Bitter, Pre-Whitsun Song" says: "Ousted, I keep walking, loitering around you. / Exiled / in my country. . . ." This separation, public as well as private, is seen again in "The Newspaper's Rustling" where the speaker says, directly, "The newspaper's rustling, they're reviling me again . . . / Today I'm just a plain plotter / in their eyes, a leader sleeping with icicles, / the planner of wars, with swans in cannon fire. . . ."

The poems in this second volume are also more apocalyptic than Csoóri's earlier work. In "Seasons at Odds with Themselves" he says, "The world is growing blind and deaf. It's less / and less concerned with what could bring about its end." And his vision has grown broader and darker, decrying the violence in the world and, especially during these more recent years, of the wars in the Adriatic and Balkan regions: "Sweet sorrow roams from the Adriatic Sea / up to the Matras Hills, from scorched forests / to the line of sickly dogwood trees, but we / can no longer give it a name." ("Seasons")

Csoóri's darkening vision is presented ironically in "Epilogue of the Dead Man." Here the speaker asserts in an understated, almost casual way, ". . . in this age / of noisy mass murders / the occasional hasty roadside slaughter / almost reassures." Just as skillfully, Csoóri uses the surreal to freight his dark vision. "Morning Awakening" features the lines " . . . your dreams are still staggering: / a horse cart in Sarajevo, loaded with corpses / and a walking, burning candle following the cart."

Regardless of his technique or poetic device, Csoóri doggedly reports the failures and horrors of his time in poem after poem. He serves as an Ishmael, an Ancient Mariner, a Whitman of the Civil War, one who sees and must pass on his vision. As long as this poet sees injustice, he will write his powerful poems, although he admits such writing will not heal him. Wonderfully, despite such knowledge, he still writes, and in such writing his spirit prevails:

> I sit, shivering,
> trying to warm up in this poem. In vain. I'm carrying
> many tiny voids inside, as if there were wounds
> waiting in me. Waiting and incurable wounds.

—Len Roberts

PART ONE
BEFORE THE FALL
POEMS FROM *MONUMENTS OF THE WORLD*
(1989)

The Day After Easter

The rooster crows the day after Easter, too,
  though you've already guessed:
    we are past every betrayal,
past our years of Peter and Judas.

We just stand here in the April garden
  among the peach trees that are to march into Heaven
    and with slitted eyes we watch
the Golgotha-like cliffs of the nearby Gellert Hill

and without words we forgive each other
  that we have lived behind doors and walls, in cellars
    studded with nails, cowardly,
in our poor, weapon-playing century

and that we have allowed lies to enter even the poems,
  the blood, the greasy pleasure
    of stroking, of killing—
And neither sword nor soldiers nor those many slobbering kissing

unmanly men have ever sickened us until today!
  As though the silver-haired
    olive trees, the oleanders
sent forth their sweet scent for someone else on the hill

and it wasn't us who stood there beneath them, white as stone
  among birds startled from their sleep,
and it wasn't us who stammered out excuse after excuse
  for the wind that dashed at us: we are nobodies,
nobodies, just the lost guests of the moon.

Injured Poem

For Ferenc Kiss, who's learning to speak after his stroke.

Let's talk, Ferenc. . . . Apple . . . Snowfall. . . .
Out in Szentendré a doe roams around your house in the snow.
It's been a while since it's seen us at the foot of Basalt Hill.
The grapes then were just beginning to glow.

Say: grape . . . honied . . . friggin'. . . .
Say: worm . . . starling . . . insolent.
Kosztolányi's hornet drifts here around our heads.
Don't fear that the thorns will skewer it.

We have already died together! Sand fell
on us from the sky and fierce shreds of shouts
from the Carpathians. Yet say that, since then

God has sent word and the Earth's ebb is slowly passing.
Say that, then: for sheer spite! slingstick and geranium scent!
Behind you: a dark shadow. Say: dark shadow.

My Masters

Where, where are my masters?
In the past they'd appear without being summoned.
They'd come before the first peal of the bells,
across barren yards: madmen, poets,
alcoholic saints; they'd come from the night's marshes,
holding Hungary's broken peony in their hands.
One of them would come with a flood,
another from between clattering tracks,
another limping, with the white frost of Bakony on his back.
And I always read the words
from their motionless lips.
Where might they linger now? Where might they be kept waiting?
With whom do they share their deaths,
the way prisoners of war share a lone potato?
As though they are ashamed
of this fouled landscape that's sunk into itself,
and their dirtied mission.

There Are Only Days

Return, return, but where?
There's no summer among the seasons any more,
no winter, no leaf-world, no beautiful, cat-eyed autumn,
there are only days: noons and evenings,
merging, dissolute mornings,
when my head and the distant seas, too, are in fragments.

Return, return, but where?
At home in the garden, the moon x-rays
the slender poppy at night, and the apple trees wait,
too, in the flickering green television light.
There, each raked place is already a strange place,
each metal-backed beetle looks like a lightning bug.

Return, return, but where?
To words? To silence? To language-solitude?
                    There are so few words
left which still stick to their own faith,
so little hope near the ram-shackled God's shadow,
so little hope for the words going from door to door,
from country to country, like howling, half-witted saints.

Return, return, but where?
Time, abducted and raped,
will not, within this town's walls, bear me a new age,
and love exposing itself in the valley will not bear me a new past.
An angry walnut leaf, about to fall, sways above, lashing the sky,
although the clouds, too, are empty, like ancient, royal,
                              looted tombs.

I Will Bear Your Slow Purification

I alone know your sorrowful sin
and I alone can forgive it, I, who have also
    slept with death.
It's July: the fiery drum sounds behind our garden
and everyone wants to see you: the way you writhe in the dust.

Even from the wild rose bushes, gloating
eyes watch. Sashegy's slope is full of them.
    They're looking at your mysterious right hand:
is the frog-scum glove of the marsh on it?
is the indelible mark?

I'm crippled. A green blackthorn ticks
timelessly by my head. But go ahead, let them see you,
    show them the deep lake of your shame,
the crazed angel drowned in it, the one who'd taken you hostage,
the one who would have taken you with himself to eternal flames.

In the morning, a high mountain-peak shines: God's lime-
white face. I don't want to look at anything else
    until you stand on your feet,
just this plateau of light. Should the stone dazzle me
    for seven weeks,
should it dazzle for seventy-seven: I will bear your slow purification

in time, lovingly, or lovelessly, I, who have suffered
greatly from others' sins repeatedly, and more greatly
    from my own. On my hand
the green blood of grass, of leaves, dries,
and the forest listens to the dull beats of my heart behind your back.

The Time Has Come

The time has come, my Lord, for me to sit out here before
        you on the hilltop.
I can see the sky's already clouding over above your church.
And in the garden growing Octobery,
my dog, too, bites your fattest roses in two,
   like cock-heads tossed on a dung heap.
       Decay organizes itself, my Lord, against us,
    it would be a mistake to deny it.
I, who wanted to survive your light in my eyes,
can see continents loaded with garbage gliding into each other
                 daily,
and indifferent empires spitting into the sea.
Smoke, smoke, poisoned dust and the gang
   of poisoned words roam among our quiet hours.
What, my Lord, will become of your waterdrops? What will
            become of your snowdew?
What will become of your psalmy bees fallen into a swoon?

Can You Still Hear It?

Pale people, days, years, pass,
can you still sometimes hear
the nervous patter of your shoes on the pavement,
and your faltering anthems?

Every acacia will bloom this year, too,
every chestnut, every dogwood.
The country-founding hand
appears above them each day in dawn's chill
and passes over them all.

Can you recognize these tireless,
willful hands among the leaves?
Can you recognize in yourself their swish?
Or do you, too, think Hungarians can have only bad luck?
Now and then I watch you while you roll along:
there are so many languished ghosts in your rows,
so many hardened-eyed people departing,
so many who listen to the music of straw-bearded summer
as though they were just listening to a beggar-Tinódi
on some street corner.

So I have a hundred reasons for talking
about you in past tense, in the voice of perishing species of birds
and caved-in wells. But you are to me
as my poetry is: a world's always born
from the pain, and an armored sky from the shame.

Pale people: days, years pass,
can you still hear in yourself the delicate echoes of their departures,
and your anthems that have been sung to death?

A Night Journey into Germany

Darkness, wind. Down the Elbe
  some huge, shapeless cargo slowly floats.
    Perhaps a vast sack.
    Perhaps a ship.
Perhaps a lost, stray mountain after an earthquake.

Outside, the night is cold,
  the water's cold,
    like totalitarian states.

All the rushing train's irons are also cold.

Withdrawn into the compartment's nook,
  with downcast eyes I'm passing alongside
    Germany's wounds.

Can you see me now, dead men's eyes,
  shooting by on the riverside?
Can you see me, bone-citizens, smoke-souls?
I should roar, like one who, after forty years,
  now wakes from among the ruins
    to the scream of red-hot beams tumbling from the sky,
and I should beat the train's window with my fist,
that the past may pass, but
    beneath my skin
      there's the memory of all the meanness
        the war bequeathed us,
here, here, like a snake in the bowl of sweets.

Bloody little skirts: front-line poppies
  and church towers shot in the head
    lie on their backs, staring at me from the ground.
And yet my hands in my lap
  do not budge for them,
my throat does not open,

as though someone had stuffed
  velvet or roses
    into my mouth.

In the countryside all around
  darkness stands in indistinct mounds.
Trees, posts, terrible-eyed eagles from empty space
    meld into it,
and my dim, passing shadow melds into it, too.

Down the river,
  that shapeless spirit of darkness floats along.
    Perhaps a swollen sack.
      Perhaps a ship.
Perhaps a lost, stray mountain after an earthquake.

I Look Back and Don't See Myself

I look back and don't see myself
young, not in the rains, not under
the snow-stuffed skies. It's autumn,
old war autumn, and I hear all the bells
of Fehérvár peal together on an ominous morning.
But now only my chest echoes with them.

Falcons drank from the river I waded through.
The water ran green over my shadow.
But where has that lean, rushing shadow gone?
And where the sedgy rim of the opposite bank?
The falcon nailed to the sky is feebly squealing,
like a thief nabbed in an earthquaky theft.

Nowhere is my bravish face. Nowhere, the warmth of my hands.
My psalm-singing mouth, too, is under ash.
As though I were the dictionary of some forgotten language,
or an ill-timed dream, where time
skips centuries, stone to stone,
and from the tops of poplars up to the moon.

I rummage in made beds, I throw pillows
aside, like the secret police drunk
with house-search, but even on the creased sheets
only the uncovered faces of women are flaming—nowhere does mine!
Maybe I, myself, was my youth's false witness—
and the fiery dogs running in the field, did I see them,
there, where a storm tumbled dry tawny stalks?
Or has it been too long since I tasted fresh, gurgling blood,
blood renewing me again for the last time,
when the salt settled in my eyes would be rinsed away,
and I could see myself once more under every sky,
in the doorway of every house, in the wind-swept garbage
of borderlands? With light-rains lashing behind my back?

Holy and Wicked Time

What another hot summer! The tinder
of forty days' drought upon us. The clods,
the ridges of hills are crumbly, and funneled
whirlwinds rise from the midst of rye fields.

Crickets and rose beetles dried flat
lie in the field, scattered on their backs,
their feet up, like herds of Ethiopian cattle
dead from thirst.

For weeks now dust, dust and ash have been drifting
from even the cemeteries. Dust, dust and ash from
the statues' mouths. The hand left out in the sun
could be the cracked, burnt hand of an Etruscan

tomb-figure. Gold and whitened bones can behold
each other thus, like lovers making passionate
love. The porcelain sky can glitter thus
and sleepwalking fires set out

toward you, to touch your skin—
Holy and wicked time! Everywhere I turn,
yellow needles from high above prick my eyes. Perhaps
I should pray for rain: let it come galloping upon us,

with flood-mane hanging to the ground, like a stud of the plains.
But instead I stick my tongue to the floor of my mouth
and mutely let the world perish in the arid blast,
and myself, too, scorched in the heat of your torrid August.

Returning Home from the Flight After the War

I came home and the house was gone.
Only ruins, too, marred the courtyard:
ends of beams, a hoe handle, a jar,
adobe clinging to adobe
      in filthy mating,
and on top of them a mirror, unbroken.

I had lived here, I had been a child here,
    the shadows with sacks had sneaked
        up into the attic here,
in fall the moon had crept through the peak-hole
and placed a candle nest to the chimney here.
The rains, the rains, taking off their white shirts,
had come home here.

What mines, shells
    and armies danced here?
What fists? The milking stool,
like a suckling, lay on its back
with dead, twisted legs.
Not a tablespoon in the dust,
not a knife, not a living plate,
not a cloud snagged on a pear bough.

Maybe animals hunted from a plane
might dream of so much chaos,
    and of so much emptiness bursting apart
      as I dreamt of there in the courtyard.
Each palm-sized bit of space was a scaffold's
memory around me. So I sat down upon a dead
section of wall, though I saw myself running,
    breathless, in the open meadow,
  among bullets, tufts of grass and spurting lumps of earth.

The Nook Was Fine for Me

The nook was fine for me, the mattressed couch,
the hat-covered lamplight
above indented beds;
it was fine for me to have a creaky sleep.

The moon, like a delayed fear of death,
often arrived to make the walking-clock's shadow,
the walls, the window frames grow,
but it was fine even to be superstitiously afraid.

Snow was falling in Paris, hail in Zámoly, and on the mountainsides
of Georgia the blood of eagles poured into the valley;
in every defeat I was a stranger, and in every mourning,
but it was fine even to be a stranger on earth.

And it was fine to walk here in the light of kind eyes,
as it was fine for that slim, radiant man
of Nazareth, too, marching into the City
on an unkempt, Palm Sunday donkey.

Drums rumbled for him in the sheep bells' quiver
like an epileptic soldier—
I have been shaken like that by the perishable bodies of my lovers,
when again and again the night awakened me to them.

Their groins were scorching, scalding,
just like the Jerusalem sand,
yet I have never thought of a rosemary-easy redemption,
but instead of long-haired warm rains even today,

that come, say goodbye, see the trains
off or the tormenting wars of nerves.
The sun comes out in their wake like immortality,
and snails set out slowly in the grass toward infinity.

Poets, My Fellows

Vainly you wail that all is lost:
countries, books, and that even the stabbed sky's
already laid out before you.
Your lamenting is worth even less
than making your bed on a snowflake for the night.

Poets, my fellows, Jeremiahs guzzling coachmen's wine,
I fidget among you in my drenched shoes
under the slushy trees of the People's Park, and I admire
the last ant marching off, about
to make the gravedigger's shovel heavy in the weighty fall.

Look, what spite even in saying goodbye!
What a spurring attention before death!
Each leaf's a country across which
that ant darkly walks. Poems and iron boots
may creak at my forehead—now I only dream of them.

May the Water Keep Vigil with Me

I wake. Outside there's a lake
and a foreign country's darkness.
Inscrutable cry of bird
under the bushes,
as though someone were being murdered.

My head's heavy with drinking,
heavy with myself. In my recent dream
shirtless soldiers were running
and combing the ruffled park
with raised pitchforks.

Were they looking for me? For you, the long-banished?
I can't remember anymore. A blood stain
shone darkly on a stone. Past that, a storm lantern,
overturned. The flame mingled with the mud
and made everything so finite, so shameless.

I'd like to sleep for spite, too. I'd like to forget
my European nightmare, the horror of those flat on their backs,
but in this foreign silence I'm just stumbling and groping;
I turn on the tap, let the water flow—
may it keep vigil with me till morning.

Forest in the Matras*

Forest,
    unfathomable, green dream,
      summer and a shadowy thrush
       hide in your bushes.
Grasshoppers eternally sunbathe
on an outlawed bone turned out of the earth.

For weeks I, too, have been your
    unfathomable story,
      I walk up and down in you shadowly,
the cracking echoes of leaves, branches keeping me company,
my hand, my fright, my voice are fragmentary;
      someone will have to
        re-dream my life.

The past taps behind my back,
      just like September's acorn, half-ripe.
Forest, forest, to me you are Dante's Wood,
       God's green prison camp—
Wherever I turn: I hear death's
    slipshod sentences from an abyss,
I see the faces of my lost turning into tree
    stumps torn up by their roots.

* The Matras, in northeast Hungary, are that country's highest peaks.

August Evening

See, a hand sweeps stars
    from the August sky,
as if my mother swept off
the supper crumbs from the table at home.
Her apron, slipping now and then, smells of parsley
    and chives—
The sweet scent of her long-gone garden
    sending me to sleep beside you tonight again.

I'd Have to Go Blind

IN THE JOYOUS MONTH OF MY LIFE—the poets of old
thus began their poems.
It was evening, the wind was blowing, the little candle flame beaten
      down.
The quince, like the memory of squandered summers,
sent its sweet scent around the room.
Knife, book, and pheasant feather lay on the table,
   and the shadow swelled
      an unredeemable skull upon the wall.

Nothing was in its place,
although everything had its place:
the thrush screeched and the swallow, seeking its homeland, twittered
in the pearly-lettered notes scattered about the ground;
gardens whispered with jasmine throats,
and lovers, too, strewing their skirts:
sweet ones! of a secret kingdom
   who, like forest fires,
      devoured the air around them.

Reeds rattled from the distance,
the grass-clodded field throbbed,
as if death had driven a black stud westward
at the hour of ghosts:
a masterless herd of horses rounded up from the battleground.
It was good then to shudder with them,
to shudder with the earth,
   and to write an entreating hymn
      to the god of the country and the war.

IN THE JOYOUS MONTH OF MY LIFE—I, too,
would begin a poem,
in a leisurely fashion, the way the sky, starting out
for a walk, saggingly snows over the Esztergom hills,

and I would listen to the cries of wild geese between the lines:
to birds screeching backwards from the war's recurring dream,
    like one who, for a long time, has not wondered why
                he's been allowed to live,
    but about having survived.

Nearby trees would stare at me,
like the exulting eyes at my birth,
and, encircling me, the hawthorn scent
of the dead soldiers buried on the hilltop
would drift. But what's the use
today of wonder and imagination
when they walk like pilgrims from the Holy Land
  into the stupid nothingness.
Winter tulips, Eskimos, people from the moon could throng
  here as well,
    my eyes would soon get used to them, too,
      as to these dried, autumn doubts.

Somewhere in the troughy valley
hunters keep banging.
Echo follows echo. Landscape-fragments, reeds covered with snow,
martyr hares in the crossed sights of the telescopes.
All is stirring, all is splintering and blood-silk tacking threads.
I'd have to go blind to see the world again,
I'd have to go deaf to hear it. The rustle of hair
  and the sea
    in a single sound,
      and the power of measured time in the din of an axe.

I'd Rather Stay at Home

I'm not leaving for your place, it's snowing again today,
the wind's lashing and there's so much, still so much snow blowing
in the valley in front of your house.
Perhaps if I had a tank, a snowplow, a horse,
perhaps if I had spiked stilts
        carved for a goliath!
From a set distance, crows would go
with me all the way, like black soldiers
        on border patrol.
But, if floundering on foot,
even the sparrows shivering on thistle stalks
would look at me as though I were a lost,
winter tourist, or
a clown bumbling-stumbling in the desert.

So I'd rather stay home in my nook-sized room,
        unromantic,
          alone,
            scorned,
and with the remorse of poets
who have grown to love comfort, I'll think of you, the wind,
the snowstorm that buries even your alarm clock,
sitting in that crowned chair
from where, the very last time, you were
smiling, bare,
at my snow-covered poplars.

Diary, Early Fall of 1982

Again this hailstorm in my hip!
Again these slanted rains before my eyes,
and this dismal spying on the earth:
who cries behind a blade of grass,
and where does the army roam?

Again these wide-open gascocks:
Iran and Lebanon burning all day long,
scorched, ghastly corpses!

And scratchy dance music
on the sea's warped record!

As if gigantic, faded canvases
were being folded from all four cardinal points:
the summer's ended—

The globe-trotting roads, like carpets, are also rolled up.

Dust and the travel-seeking, yellow dogberry leaves
sit by my side wearily,
gazing with empty mummy-faces
straight ahead into the afternoon.

It Will Remain My Living Memory

I'm here with you
    and right now it's good to be with you.
A butterfly's on the stone, on its wings the burning eyes of a peacock:
perhaps the billboard of summer,
or perhaps of your eyes.

Your body murmurs quietly beside me,
    as though a radio played lowly.
Your breathing's received by grass-antennas.
And a grass-herd of horses rushes toward you,
and the green flood of a hundred-acre wheat field from the hill,
and the fantasy of our being swept away
still pleases me now, as it always has.

I'll see you here and there in the villages,
    on writers' evenings, or beneath the bunned linden trees.
Cries and long curses flow from the theater,
but from every tale there, too,
you'll run away
and by the side of unknown men
you'll follow the crazed, frenzied sounds of May.

Already I feel it: I will have to pulse with the pain
    that you were,
and that you won't lie beside me anymore on the lake shore, in the hill grass,
and that it won't be me in your dreams
who will brush grayed ladybirds off your body.

It will be good for me to watch a long time
the inviting bout of your beautiful breasts:
it will remain my living memory,
my model for every death.

Late Winter Morning

We're here and everything that can help us
to live today is still here, too:
the wind rushing along the quays,
the heavy sighs bursting from the trees,
and a gull circling low
over the Danube. It floats, it pauses,
keeps busily counting
the deathly ice floes that float toward Belgrade.
And your green eyes, which cast
this day ashore, are also here.
Green, green, green—the numb
augurs just keep gaping under the cold sky;
they would like to utter aloud
the leaves' green, the lilac's green,
and the lettuce's green leafing in the soft rains,
so it wouldn't be me who'd have to dream them again.

In the Summer, I Can Hear a Clatter of Hooves

I start out, and I still don't know where I'm going.
Maybe this restless lime tree will help me
make up my mind: suddenly
it bends into the wind
and flies before me up the hill,
after the hornets galloping away,
bees that keep assaulting the valley
  with the gold-trimmed flag
of sweetness and fierceness,
evoking saber-bearing centuries'
warriors of the border fortresses.
The always-cheated blood in me—
time stuck at the foot of castle ruins—
    flares up at their sight
as if lurking defiance
and the rapture of raids had reared me
even before my birth!
From Esztergom I can hear screams and a clatter of hooves
in the summer: Mary, Mary, Our Mighty Lady, help us!
    I can see: stirrups brushing weeds,
        hissing nettle
and blood-covered eyes soar over my head:
cannonballs shelled at virgins.

I bend down on the wind, too, as on a horse's neck,
and blindly I let myself be carried on blood's path.
Butterflies scamper away from me,
westward, afraid,
with my heartbeat and my shame.

I Wanted to Arrange

I wanted to arrange everything:
dreaming, waking, a cool tree leaf
    on the hot mouth,
and a long, happy laugh into the dull alley.
And the crimes of day-laboring death
committed in the heat of anger and passion. But now I just
pace from tree to tree, from street corner to street corner,
    like an anxious madman,
and I bite into the wind, the mountains: let me finally know:
are there still mountains, and from those mountains does the
    wind still blow?

The Missed Roads

for András Sütö[1]

My God, those many missed roads
up to Kolozsvár! I could travel in my dreams
around the earth on them. Yellow furze-light
and nights growing gloomy with buffaloes' bulging eyes
would move from town to town before me.
Passes, churches, wooden bridges and the shoes
of suicides scattered in the forests would come
with me as jostling ghosts. And Ady's[2] shadowy hat,
pulled well over a star's forehead,
covered the countries ahead with darkness.
A pilgrimage? A road of shame? Lonely
funeral procession on the earth pricked full with bloody souls?
With a glittering gold coin between my teeth
I'd search for the cemeteries that had been carried off
and would make the dead speak whispering from beneath the earth
about the heads severed by axes, since it's true now
that barren raw chalk creaks in the mouths of the living
instead of words. . . . My God, those many missed roads
and missed rustle of leaves to Kolozsvár! that
bend-marking brilliant furze-light on the Királyhágo[3]
ledge! I truly don't know: would there still be a road
to take me there? Or does even the grass-covered
path lead up to only the old hearts, where there are as many stones
as in the bed of the Sebes-Körös[4] under Csucsa[5]?

[1] András Sütö: a Transylvanian prose writer and playwright.
[2] Endre Ady: a famous Hungarian poet who wrote at the end of the nineteenth and
    beginning of the twentieth centuries.
[3] Királyhágo: pass connecting the Great Hungarian Plain with Transylvania.
[4] Sebes-Körös: a river in Transylvania
[5] Csucsa: a castle-village in Transylvania.

So You Won't Be a Witness Today Either

Anything, even an exhausted wink,
  a look askance,
    a careless side-glance at the clouds, the lilacs
is enough for you not to be a witness today, too,
not to see the indifferent bullets soaring through
your room,
the green stable of worms near your woman's face,
not to see yourself in another,
nor in yourself, either;
a little eye-tango in the blue,
a shred dance of the pupil is enough
to make gardens,
    gables,
      roofs tilt,
        tiles redly tremble,
to make you see the skin of ancient mummies also quivering
as though they were living,
as though light were rushing all about them,
haranguing you even from the glass coffins,
you, who can't tell for yourself: are these
  voices you hear,
is your hand,
    this wind,
      this summer with the trembling of long trees
  all just in your memory
or have you grown to be the earth's souvenir, perishing,
a muddled body among the timbers, in weeds,
and here in the site of your heart
there's only your left side, aching—

Monuments of the World

The tramping time comes and goes,
   and I, too, walk about the snow-covered town.
The streets, like crumbling lead-lines
    of a poem that's been set in type,
    watch me inconsolably.
The monuments of the world darken
     in me from minute to minute then,
and I hear the sound of hoarse flutes
above stone flags and bronze lions
    and marble angels descending for the war dead.

At such times I feel: you, too, would
    mark me for a victim,
  for a living, moving sidewalk-being,
    one who will march again instead of you
with demonstrative, purple leaves in the circusy autumn,
    and whose blood will be smeared
      on the Parliament's dome.

But I have been an elusive, moving fire
    for a long time, my friends,
     a moving will, a freed hope,
    and I am not to be sacrificed again
   without my assent.
In my mouth the bitterish tastes
    of autumn revolutions, autumn screams and asters,
    and above me, street lamps lighting, one after the other.

In the Grape Dropped on the Sidewalk

A beautiful autumn again this year, sunny November,
   but only the old idled everywhere,
moved slowly in the bright sunshine,
      like fists shelling corn.
With eyes downcast, I walked among them in the park, the boulevards.
I didn't want them to see: it is only
   your repeatedly blooming body
      that reminds me of mortality.
Even in the grape dropped on the sidewalk, I look for it—
maybe in the street scene of your sweet movement,
      I can catch sight of it—
your smile conniving with the sky,
      encircled thickly with the scum of dead-yellow leaves.

Among the Ferns of Finland

Here, now, I've got plenty of time,
    it doesn't press;
fate doesn't hiss at me from the underworld grass.
Two giant stones watch me: two red oxen,
sprawled out on the shore, as if just chewing their cuds.

It's not even noon,
    yet two showers and five stray sea gulls
have already dropped in on me.
The gulls came like sailors on leave from Helsinki,
leaving the sky behind them white with scribbling.

Far from here, in the city,
    gold watches throb nervously
and fifty million half-mad wheels revolve in the street,
revolve in the ground, above the ground,
in the bowels of machines, and the academy

of glistening nickel-brains
    shakes with dry crying:
where are those wheels running, and for what?
where the passions, in blue-enameled cages?
And can Man stem again the ancient wounds

if he wants to,
    by old-fashioned, blissful tumult,
the way roes, butterflies, deer
and poets condemned to extinction can pause
by a huckleberry bush?

Or is he to drift
    in an idyllic way toward the rays of death,
along the path of poisoned needles
and fire-branded missiles,
accompanied by imperial ear-ringing music?

Nothing, nothing. I'm conceding:
    let the doubts, the desires run on,
let the dazed wheels run.
Lying among the ferns of Finland, I listen:
the forest is talking to itself; old, very old, it talks.

You Look at Me Like

You look at me like
   I'm a would-be assassin,
      one who throws stones at the swans
in the town park's lake
and buries alive the nightingale.
If you had a God,
before going to sleep
you'd complain to him, blushing, about me,
but since you don't, you just hunch your shoulders,
      you just stare from the stiff hoop of your collar
at my solitary walks under the sky.
The cars stream out from the sunshine,
weapons, cries stream,
the nettle is torn from the earth;
still you whisper with a drafty mouth
behind my back: isn't this world my fault?
   isn't it I who has clandestine dates
with the blazing thought of death?

Large, sluggish curtains draw apart
   and noiselessly close,
eyes, unknown even under the clouds, throng:
      they'd like to know who I am.
Nobody, nobody—I'd like to comfort them—
just the memory of an unstoppable, demonstrating crowd
marching like a voiceless procession from street to street,
the concrete behind it tapping,
time tapping.

Young Nuns of Rome

I can see the young nuns of Rome
  moving off toward the Tiber.
Their blue-linen skirt-dresses,
like a punch's black-and-blue bruise circling a woman's eye,
     keep smarting in the morning.
Butterflies set out lazily to follow them
   from the wet fountain-rim
and sighing centuries from below the Castel Sant' Angelo.
O Lord, O Lord, I, too, mutter to myself,
  watching the cracked concrete,
what heavenly knees
   and breasts blessed with mercy
     pass away from the world aimlessly.

As Blue-Flamed Butterflies with the Prodigal Son

Alone at last. Nine in the morning.
In the world at last, myself a world, too.
In my memories, there's not a profile, a palm, not one mad snowfall
which would now blot out the roofs.
And nobody's weeping,
either, in the cold stairwell.

The victims of my fidelity and infidelity
might be seeking each other right now in town,
to glorify me and damn me.
The telephone rings, the artificial ears ring
in the wall, but I am not there now,
where it's a custom to kill with words.

On my table, a thin strip of light is flickering;
deceptively, it sways to the right, to the left,
as my poplars are bent by the wind.
Minutes pass swiftly until I understand:
the world is playing with me,
as blue-flamed butterflies played with the prodigal son.

Have I, too, come home, then?
tousled, prodigal son, home, into myself?
Someone who's been laughing for three days
still walks there, along the sand of the red-shot
ocean shore. Carob beans hung
brownly from the trees and I no longer
wanted to be other than light, light,
who talks with God, with the summer!
Today, only the vista of towns and waters is looming,
and even that is a lightning-struck anarchy.
And, facing San Francisco, an ant from back home is creeping,
silence growing behind it, as my watch ticks.

Russet roofs ripple before me
in the morning. I'm depressed by the white window-grille's geometry.
Yet, inside me, I'm free
as no one else can be. I'm what infinity
wishes to be: a face that's awakened to itself,
and the site of ecstatic expectations, again and always.

If You Were God's Relative

And the day will come, when your gurgling mouth
    won't want to speak anymore
and your eyes won't want to see themselves
        in the familiar mirror,
because there will have been so much smoke, filth,
rain bounding upon bloody legs on the earth,
so many dim marks on the winners' faces,
        so many, too, on the losers',
and your eyes finally will have grown tired of mercy,
    of delivering justice from one sinner to another—

If you were God's relative, you would now be stepping
    through winter's cracking walls of glass,
        just as if you were marching in a fog,
you'd hug a tree, a woman
and you'd demand your dead friends back from the cemeteries:
"Return them to me, Earth,
        for without them
        I can no longer judge myself."
You'd walk, ready for a miracle,
    on the ground of the people-eclipsed homeland,
        and from beneath the forests, pheasants—
the decorously dressed Indians of your childhood—
    would shriek toward you.

Courtyard at Home, Before Autumn

September. In the courtyard, long sunlight
and faded hollyhocks in front of the kitchen wall.
A lame blister-beetle
limps between them toward the night.
Rain, lightning
and the unharnessed horses' shadows
set out slowly after it
into long exile.
I know, you'd set out with it, too,
fleeing from fall,
fleeing from winter,
into yourself, inward:
on dim, green roads,
where no hoar-frosted bell-peal and clock-stroke
has ever gone with you.
But you must learn at last
to stay here at this place
of ruin: on the land
of leprous walls and snapped-off door handles,
beside the rims of badly sleeping wells,
for even in the courtyard here at home
you are the only one,
a profile springing up high,
Jonah remembering
the decaying village-Ninevehs.

Even now fat flies buzz
around the yawning stable-mouth,
as they'd buzzed about the smeared mouth
of the girl born mad.
The roots of their soft wings
are churning
the sludge of honey and jam,
of sturdy dung heaps.
Even though they once

made your young stomach heave,
today their black
band plays music
for the dead horses
buried beneath the crib.

The lame blister-beetle limps
in front of the deserted sties.
Behind it, in the courtyard's aged dust,
little, tiny whirlwinds stir.

PART TWO
AFTER THE FALL
POEMS FROM *WITH SWANS, IN CANNON FIRE*
(1994)

Wandering in a Former Party Office Building

Doors open in front of me again,
and I walk through huge, gray halls.
Everything's the same: the doorstep, the chandelier,
even the historical murals.
But in the nooks, here and there, hands ripped
from wrists seem to appear, dusty interrogation lamps
and faint blood on the floor. I don't understand:
how could blood get here? How could scrotums
tied off with string get here?
When I was a young man here years ago: silk strings
with bobbles hung from curtains. What's happened
since? The corners, window-recesses,
the huge pits under the mahogany desks
are stuffed with body stumps? Wherever I step
I now can see between the extolled walls
there's not one inch of space
where some crime against my imagination
hasn't been committed. There's not one
carved ornament that remained innocent
on the cabinets. Oh, dear God, dwarfish executioners
drank here, too, from the cut
crystal glasses; for years they swilled
vodka and their croaking, piggish anthems with reddening faces.
The floor groans, the door slams—a strange dream
is wasping around me. Or is it only the late fancy
of the flesh that's been terrorized so often?
That of the uncrowned witness who believed himself
guilty for the guilty ones, too?
Outside I hear poplar-threats and inside
a clock that's broken free strikes twenty-five. Who knows
what kind of calendar will begin again tomorrow?

Sometimes I Watch Her

She's coming, and with her comes the Esztergom sunshine
on the backs of twenty butterflies. And a whole line
of poplars from Kolozsvár and twelve bells.
Because they want to live there, where she opens the door
and smiles at the one who's arrived.

Sometimes I watch her: her hands flutter
among reveling wasps, as if she were playing the violin
with summer's glass bow for them. I can't help
keeping my eyes glued on her,
keeping my life on her.

Backbiters, meanwhile, whisper she's guilty,
like every woman: she wants a world
for her companion: a traveling dust mote,
a house, an ocean for a deckchair.
But if you see my walking shadow with her
marching up the hill: forgive every lover.

In Filtered Shade

Who are those well-groomed beer drinkers
there in the garden above Pasaret
beneath a huge sun umbrella?
On their necks, thick, hammered gold necklaces,
and their hairy fingers,
like fat bumblebees,
flutter lazily
above each glass.

Unknown, like little Columbuses,
who have each just recently
discovered
a land swimming in haze
with banana plantations,
with green apples,
with ant farms,
and they already ship
barrels of formic acid
to armies secretly arming themselves.
Or they trade women at bargain rates
for classical ruins.

In the filtered shade and in the gray
cigarette smoke they are like those
who can see without eyes,
who can hear without ears,
and who can feel with their slumbering temple-veins:
where pearls roll from the seas
and blood from the tapped bodies.

Borders? Borders? Torturing dispersals?
Poor hymns, hiding homelessly?
And the wild, pacing falcons
on Bartók's nearby statue-head
seem to them as distant as the flutist of death.

Leaning against a tree, I'm watching
their bumblebee fingers flitting in the afternoon.
I can see they own
this day, as well as the sky.
Who can say it's not the hearts
of my new torturers growing stronger in them?

The Citizen of the Garden

I don't want to leave
this garden: not for banquet halls, nor
city halls, nor the seashore.
The Colosseum in Rome is just a gangrenous
sunflower, and the lampposts of London
are ineradicable weeds. Here even
the twisted blade of grass is more alive:
it whispers to the grasshoppers, to the temple
of the dog sliding on its stomach. Not to mention
the orchids, the wild carnations, the field poppies!
They butterfly-race with the white silkworms,
lap after lap, race with death.

I've seen everything that I had to see on earth:
the colorful fan of countries from
great heights, in sweltering summer,
and the cellophane-rustling cities. But never
the hearts of grasses or the hearts of shadows.
Nor the heart of God dying every day.

If I left here again, I know
I'd lose eternal things. I'd be a wound
infected by scratching, a wound
that travels wretchedly, a wound
in which orphans of shelled villages are ringing the bells.

On the nameday of Sarolta, the elderberry
drops its white plates on my chest. Even my bones
ring quietly then. I listen to this instead
of the clamor of cannons and farewell zithers,
this, this sound rippling out
and the walking rose-bug's hum.

I Rip a Blade of Grass in Half

In the garden I walk and walk,
but there's no hillock where I might sit,
only a hill, only a hill
peopled with butterflies and needlegrass.
My God, God, so I've lived to see this too!
I can sit high above here, near you,
and rip blades of grass in half. Grass
and worlds. On one side the golden orioles
and the everblooming evil-doers
are bustling, and on the other, those
who flare like matchsticks. And those
who betray them. And those who kill.
What a disgrace, yes, a disgrace: this is what has become
of the green, the blue, the red whirling masterpiece
of the drama of waters and splitting stones,
this, this nerve-withering mish-mash, this,
this human race married to the morass.
I know all too well, though, that you don't yell
like a toothless, callous lush, from the sky
or from inside the mountain of clay.
And that with strict patience you must wait,
wait with me a long time on the mountaintop,
marking my forehead with the green grass's blood.

Etching of a Small Town

Get out of here, I'm telling you, get out,
this isn't a tavern reeking of garlic
with some bartender's railed counter, where
you can tear every poster off the wall and ogle
at weevils. Take a good look around,
everything's in its place: the brass door handle,
the brass tap, the brass mortar, and you could
even find room for the screaming of feeble animals.
And the clock! The cuckoo clock! It throbs
as if the mayor's heart had been laid out
on parade. . . . Get out, I'm telling you,
get out. Even your breathing
is monitored, as though you were in intensive care.
Should you cry out just once, just once talk about
the multiplying, red spiders
so someone might overhear, or about
the dogs devouring the guest flesh, your linen shirt
will be snatched at once, your mouth stuffed with clouds,
feathers of swans, and you'll turn blue with them,
like the worm-eaten plums of June.
Are you writhing? Are you twitching?
There might still be some of your sheriff's deputy-henchmen
in town who will strap you in the eau de Cologne straitjacket.
Get out of here, I'm telling you, get out.
The musk scent of geraniums is too intense.

Sunday Still Life—with Table, with Knife

After six days, when the seventh
marches into my home
like a helmetless army of reserves,
I will have been lying a long time,
full length, on the cold kitchen floor,
and from my temple, instead of lukewarm
blood, only tiredness will ooze.

To the right of my face
a square, wan table leg
is towering. To the left:
a big knife dropped after a killing.
And, as though close by, a turkey
and goose-throat were wailing,
or a silky-skinned piglet.

Maybe, though, it's not the weak
animals rasping at me,
but the days. My days: Monday
and Tuesday and Friday flayed alive,
the stork-legged Saturday,
which has stalked in thick marsh
up to its hocks and now cannot fly.

What could happen today
has happened to us before:
instead of tanks, loud circus vans
tore up and down the cities' streets
for weeks, stopping only now and then
outside the morgues
so we would not forget our fear.

Even from down here on the kitchen floor
I can see them darting. And I can see
the clowns making faces: they're explaining

with split mouths that no crime
can be resolved until we at least dream
about the murderers. But the tall rows
of houses just echo the mocking laughter.

My Sunday head is again
like a hard quince-apple that's fallen off
the cupboard and will continue its descent
because of its own weight. Down, down
into a sacred space where there no longer is
a table leg, or knife, or hands, just
voices, signs, just long-drawn-out bell-peals
and music keeping time to the march of earth ants.

Where Are My Betters Who Fell Behind?

Incomplete sonnet

Where are my betters who fell behind:
the swishing-brains, the saints,
the half-crazed inventors who send
messages with green-backed, bright bugs to the moon?

Perhaps they, like the silk princes,
ramble between seas and islands?
or they sleep with Greek ruins,
behind the gods' lazy eyelids?

Why don't they drink their beer
by the kennel wall, where the dog
guards the geniuses' skulls. Here, here,

where the hearts daily fall flat on their backs
and the children learn the death-alphabet
in the dust from fools and poets?

Seasons at Odds with Themselves

It's fall, just take a good look at the bushes,
    where no thrush is frisking.
You can see through their branches,
    as through the walls of razed houses.
Not one boisterous harvest is to be found, not one tapping of vats,
not one funny, hoarse shepherd's horn,
just the torpid, canned music and shrieks from the radio.

The swallows left long ago,
    they took the coffins with them,
for once again we have too many dead among us,
too many even for the fatherland. Abandoned
war hands and legs are rising from the shrouds—
God, what do you do with the hands and coffins
migrating to the South?

Before our very eyes season after season is at odds
    with itself. We kick rusty iron
instead of rusty fallen leaves.
Sweet sorrow roams from the Adriatic Sea
up to the Matra Hills, from scorched forests
to the line of the sickly dogwood trees, but we
    can no longer give it a name.

The world is growing blind and deaf. It's less
    and less concerned with what could bring about its end.
I walk from tree to tree: can I still trust them?
Does their skin tremble from my hand,
like the skin of tamed foals? Or are they, too,
just our bad memories,
    like the centuries lugged into museums?

Biographical Fragment

I lived with an old, thin Jew
on Csengery Street in fifty-four.
He was a sad, seal-eyed bachelor
who the hookers called "my Gézuka."

Only smoke, smoke and crows in overcoats
came to see us
and cats reminiscent of fat Margot.

He was driven by hopelessness,
I was driven by hope to move to Pest,
and, halfway, we met. If he'd lifted a finger then:
his dead, in slaked-lime uniforms, with rust-tinted hands
would have stolen back
and opened every door before him.
But instead of calling them he gazed
at his worn shoes beside his bed
as though into the mouth of an everyday mass grave.

When he hummed a tune, I knew he wanted to howl
and tear the leaves off trees with hairy Isaiah-hands.
Hunyadi Square darkened quickly then
and frightened flocks of screeching jenny wrens fled
from the kindled lamps toward the Ukraine.

If I'd been a sailor,
a priest or God,
he would never have shared his room with me,
but because I once wrote a poem in the salt
that had settled on the back of my hand, like sea gulls on a crag,
he considered me immortal
and made me tea in the whistling kettle.

I was his living companion but all his dead
ones, too. Young brother of the strangling angels.
He trusted my disheveled mop of hair
more than Samson did his own.

Clumsy twin brothers: we'd often hang out
on Heroes Square, as yet unregistered
victims of the betrayed future.
Sometimes a swan limped toward us
from under the trees by the Városliget pond,
blood trickling from its left eye
onto the filthy ground.

February Vision

Fifteen years after László Nagy died

Who's dawn-dancing on your grave,
László? No joke, even his ankles
are covered with frost. His teeth, his nape,
his hungover fists. But he is stamping, stamping
the wicked clay with his feet, as if
he wanted your temples, as if
he wanted that other space, opening in the place
of your heart, where sloe-planets
and silver pocketwatch-moons revolve.
Through bare branches and through fine mist
I'm staring at this bumptious bum,
this graveyard gigolo-dancer who's singing,
who's neighing, who's clicking and tossing
kisses to the crows watching from a distance.
Even his long, nicotine-stained fingers
dance with him in the fog. The thought
of the fruitless worm standing upright
on his feet—shook me. Maybe even he
envies your death and your honeyed, courting words
that always made the supple-fleshed ladies
yield milk. . . . László, can you hear
this dawn stomping at all? This hate-dance?
The clapping of frosty legs and indigo-blue
palms? Or is it just me, me who hears it,
who's sent every day an end-of-the-world message?

Bicycle Racers

Where are you swishing, reckless cyclists,
in this freckled fall?
Chestnuts plop before you on the road,
and Balkan bullets.
Your wheels are rolling wildly
like this madly revved-up century,
and where you're racing to,
spokes are grinding, one after another,
the splendid cemeteries.

Do you know there are no more
peace marches and peace rallies?
No bay wreathes with ribbons streaming to the sea
to hang around the neck—
only deep wounds big
as bomb craters scab
the human eyes lined up along the roads,
and in the browned fields
where veering planes are forced
to continually circle by an unextinguishable dream.

Slow down, sprinting boys,
you green- and yellow-shirted strangers.
Don't drag the white steam
of your breath to a war-stricken country.
The falling chestnuts are
beautiful brown eyes:
warm brown, like the eyes of mellow women
who open the door.
I've seen every fall with them
on the gold-laced hills and, so far, every eclipse.

If This Were Life

If winter's already in even your eyes,
snowstorm and icicles on the overturned table,
I'll warm up a little in this poem.
You come and go, you're in a hurry,
death trips you up in the revolving
door's narrow cell, but
you don't even see him anymore, like those
who have sold their eye-pupils in some Balkan market stall.

There was a time when we could even be cold
together. All twenty of our nails
spent the night outside in the Hörtöbagy snow.
The movie camera was rolling, the tassels
on dark shawls were fluttering, hoar-frosted, between the farms,
and with our backs to the night, with our frosted napes,
we knew: infinity was there behind us.

A world that was but isn't. The hearts have since grown rheumatic.
Deeply wounded words and injured revolutions
lie around unburied beneath the skin—
and only the dogs now can gobble them.
If this were all life could be, ok, I'll accept it.
But if there were more? If we should have stood
in the brilliance of another thousand window-flashes of lightning
for a country, for ourselves, and we just slunk
away with wooden faces. Who's going to shake us
for this? Who's going to rip apart the faded
Viennese shirts on our chests? I sit, shivering,
trying to warm up in this poem. In vain. I'm carrying
many tiny voids inside, as if there were wounds
waiting in me. Waiting and incurable wounds.

Godless Summer

Even the dog just stands, stands and pants,
too lazy even to lie down under the bush.
Its black coat sizzles and frizzes hair by hair
as if a match flame were singeing its tips.

The grass shrivels, the elder, the blind-nettle;
wherever I look, I see little,
white skeletons staggering in the air,
and the plum-pit-sized hearts of birds fallen in the dust.

I'm afraid to look toward you, too: are your eyes
still green, can that well, glittering deep below,
linking me with the memory of seas, be seen in them?

Or are you, too, withering in this churlish summer,
yellowing like the acacia whose strength has been rent,
leaving you as nothing, just a crusted no-trespassing sign for butterflies,
        bugs?

Widows Danced

What an era ours was!
What a century! Widows
flat-chested as jackdaws
and fat as kneaded bread
danced with sad smiles, hand in hand,
to the blaring music of the ballroom bands.
The kettledrum's cymbal
    now and then tilted
        behind them like a full moon
drifting above military cemeteries.
No one wailed in the rooms anymore,
    the lights just went out now and then.
The widows kept dancing nevertheless,
    they danced in the dark,
        they danced in their worn sandals
           and shoes,
the waxed floor moaning spasmodically under them,
moaning the way, in a weedy ditch,
a man shot in the stomach might.

I, Too, Might Have Been

I, too, might have been a drunken
dirty frontline soldier: a rum hero whirling
his arms and aimlessly shooting, a rum soldier,
death's close friend, who walks around
in a cocked helmet and tickles with his bayonet
the stomachs of curled-up hedgehogs and trembling women,
then skewers the quince-apple
so he, too, has a moon.

Everything was set: sky, earth,
draft call, lustful drumbeat, the endless
roads were set. The newest dictionary
of the dead, where several words
lie for bone and lost eye.
Mother-cry in the darkened house
was set, too, there where the warm biscuits
and hot spoons would have started out
toward the snowfields every night.

Even now I hear the clattering
of trains racing in flames,
the huge, palm-sized wounds crawling through
the forest, still looking for me
from tree to tree. Where did I fall behind?
Where behind the lice: those orderlies
of the perfect, little death?

Was an angel watching over me? Was it the scabies-
infected nurse or pampered Blind Fate?
Or someone among the perishing gods,
who secretly closed every door on me
and arrayed me in bell-peal?
The bell's still ringing, ringing in me,
but I can't stop dreaming about rooms grown sooty,
and fluttering bloody swans caught in cannon fire.

Morning Awakening

Good morning—I greet you when you open
the door, and with my greeting the scent
of elderberry, of thyme, of a hundred herbs
pours into your room.
Look, the new day's guests,
I'd go on, playfully waking you
in the luster above the doorstep,
but I can see: on your eyes' green screen
your dreams are still staggering:
a horse cart in Sarajevo, loaded with corpses,
and a walking, burning candle following the cart.
It sends cold shivers down my back:
it's only me who dreams
such stageable horrors
like an ocean sated
with shipwrecked corpses.
Can it be that we
are also sharing our dreams,
like our hands, our legs?
and we slip into each other's depths
swimming, floating, with closed eyes,
stripped to nerves beneath the skin?

January Apparition

Where is last year's snow?
Where is this year's?
January gleams cold
like a scoured
limestone statue in the graveyard.
I throw black clods
at the winter trees
instead of snowballs.

I am blue, blue,
parched blue, inside and out,
and stiffening with cold I remember
staggering, drunken reed-harvesters
who made pitchforks dance on the ice
and yelled, jumping all around:
mad land, mad land.

At least five grains of frost
would roll here quickly,
at least five grains of pearls
from northern native countries.
I would multiply them
as Jesus did the fish,
I would multiply them
as Jesus did the bread.

But only a bobbing-necked gander
with ruffled feathers
is stepping whitely toward me.
He's ambling down from the tall roost.
Purple flashes of lightning keep
leaping from his waxed beak.
I stop and stare:
this goose, too, could be a castrated swan!

Where is last year's snow?
And my God, where is this year's?
Where are the tongues of the snow-covered
sleighbells and where the carnival yells?
A sparrow pecks frozen
breadcrumbs from the ground,
and flies away with one, like
a skeletal alien, filled with fright.

You Are Free, Almost Guiltily Free

Incomplete sonnet

Everyone's given up on you.
You are free, almost guiltily free. You may live
under any of God's trees or in the cellar
of a collapsed house. Your bed may be a mattress

or Mr. Heine's coveted silk bed.
Another time, a wagonful of lilies.
It wasn't you who wanted it like this, but if this
is life's price: don't moan, don't cry, say this,
too, you'll learn to live with.

Don't just say it—sing it with bared teeth:
let every vinestick split
alongside its splinters, and let your well-educated

executioners' craniums crack with them. But don't let
anyone ever tell them: there's a new age coming: the victims
will find themselves again and the pursuers will wither from migraines.

Metamorphosis in Stockholm

The winter wind's shoving
the royal statues around
in Stockholm's inner harbor.
It's carrying snow, gulls
and litter to their majestic feet.
The city's quiet, though, like the splendid dead.
Reluctantly, it follows even me,
the foreigner, with its cold, Sunday eyes.
It doesn't suspect
I'd have you keep me warm
between the centuries-old swords
and swinging masts
along its windy streets.
You or somebody else
who would be you, mostly you
through a forty-eight-hour soul-and-body swap.

Who would I admit it to,
if not precisely to you,
that for days I've mistaken
every woman walking toward me for you?
And not just the little, gypsy-black-haired ones,
not just the green-eyed
daydreamers who dance even
on the shards of glasses
hurled to the floor
as though they danced on broken snow,
or on five tons of scattered butterfly wings.
The blond ones, the light-brown ones,
the candle-thighed ones rushing to church,
the ones floating their scarves up high,
the royal whores, too, they all
approach to the cadence of your compassion.

Above, clouds: snow sails;
below, ice orchids in the water
and frozen sweat-masts.
Fearing, I think today that I am Gauguin in the North,
the man banishing himself,
the one who's looking for his own, new country
in women's breath
instead of sunshine, palm trees, islands.

Remembering November, 1956

It was fall, fall for days, weeks,
maybe years: police squad fall.
On street corners the wind
forced every homelessly wandering
tree leaf and helmeted chestnut
to prove their identity.
And the wind checked mine, too,
while I shivered with cold
in a light, spring overcoat
near Boráros Square like a blanketed
frost-bitten fugitive in the borderland.
I was weaponless,
no flag,
no knife,
not even an informing monument-fragment,
but the names and faces
of revolutionaries executed
outside Márie Therése Barracks
were hidden beneath my skin.
Someone had only to yell
from high above: Halt! Who goes there?
and with what funereal leaflets
are you walking about in this ruined city?
Maybe one marksman-finger aimed at me
would have been enough.
Enough, enough, and I would have confessed
right then that I looked just
like every most-wanted corpse
of the martyr-country,
and in vain I would leave
for the south or the north:
but there's no way out of myself.
There's no way, nowhere—

even in the poems
muddy tanks and undermined
scabrous rose-gardens block my path.

It's as if cellophane-wings
were crackling in the wind
and razor blades crunching
under boots.

Who forgot then to yell
at me there in the fall?
Who failed to bring closer
my prophesied death?

Flying Above Thirty Thousand Feet

Only sky, sky, only dispiriting
sunshine all around, and the reflected lights
of Greenland on your traveling face. And
clouds, clouds everywhere on God's abandoned
playground. Not one stirring
tatter of clothes, branch, stalk of straw, cross,
not one madly rolling train wheel
in the air, if not solely in this poem,
which has been traveling with me for seven hours.
Don't you hear it? Buzzing like a bug in the vineyard.
Like a wasp in a stone church. A minute ago
it was still teetering on the tip
of the plane wing and now it imitates a river's
gurgle, high up, here. Even if I shoo it away,
it flies back and cuddles on your lap
in a chestnut-leaf mask as if it were fall in Esztergom,
early fall, an afternoon dropping leaves,
where, even poemless, I am your
unmockable poet among the hills,
the knight of the slowly yellowing trees,
and that of the lights, too—and it's not me
who has himself transported to see the world in slender planes;
not me who's reminded of the last journey
by every journey he takes.
Do you know where we are? No? Neither do I.
Perhaps in the heart of a swan drifting to the South?

After Easter, Easter Once Again

I'm overgrown by grass, by colza, by spinach.
I'm peering out from them,
    from this killing summer,
        for the sake of others.
High up, in my space, falcons are proudly circling,
their mauve-colored livers growing bigger with gloating.

My flesh, too, once used to blaze,
not just my hair. And I was not afraid
    to sell myself
        to a flower girl.
And now earwig-ants walk over me
and I can hear them singing quietly.

No, no. Better the lap of speechless ashes
or the cruel resurrection:
    after Easter, Easter once again!
        Knives, flowers between my fingers
and church steeples towering like leaves of grass
that grow to the sky here, too, in my garden.

You, who knew all of my lives, come visit me
and touch me like a tree leaf.
    I am no more than it,
        and no less:
I rustle, I sway, I teach myself to speak again:
my mouth, my legs, all ten of my hands.

I Can See Their Eyes

I can see their eyes: blue, brown, black,
I can see them as in a rearview mirror—
as if time had stopped in them.
Scarves, shawls, heads of hair are pitching and rolling
in the bewildering whirl of boulevards,
but the motionless eyes ask each morning:
who are we? where are we hurrying?
whose world do we watch day to day?

I can see the eyes, I can see the blood in them, too,
the wheel spokes of hearses with muddy leaves,
the marble forest reprimanded
and the glinting memory of bullets
of a war re-imagined again till I'm sick of it,
and the eyes ask: how many more journeys till the last?
how many snowfalls? how many unhemmed, end-of-July nights?
how many stacks of leaves and pleatable lights?

I can see the eyes: blue, brown, black,
up, up they shoot to the sky where they wander
like beggars at trampled shrines.
The wind hauls garbage on them, dirt from below,
whisking up the world's smoke,
and the reddening eyes motionlessly ask:
is there a world beyond this world?
beautiful, frivolous moons—or just empty space?

I can see the eyes and I see myself in them:
the absence of another pair of eyes to link
me to the heart of a bush, to a shadow with prophecies.
If they moved, I'd move with them,
toward the north or south, away from under these husks
of cities scattered with stars to the peak of the night,
where two pairs of eyes would watch each other till they've had enough,
two pairs of eyes: each other's guests becoming God.

I Don't Deny It: My Eyes Are Darker

Here, together, we're still embarrassed
with each other, friends, and with what's happening
during this summer that's gone up in flames
like a silk scarf. One keeps coming and going,
yelling among us, leaning his elbows on a knife;
one nervously munches apple cores
and searches the cemetery for his lost
coat button. And there's one who
senses the scent of the Midsummer Night's donkey
hide wafting from the direction of Parliament,
and he flees, flees.

So this is what we get, the truly laughable
one-time winners—in defeat?
These platitudes, clumsy stories?
I can see the fancy handkerchiefs at half-mast,
they're fluttering one by one above
your temples as though in an abortive love.
Only those times of lying low on the shadow horses
and in the shadow cars of the eternal Bakony Hills are missing.
Only the sleeping pills dissolving in brandy,
and Bartók, even when played on a comb, wailing.

A wagon loaded with seaweed is just now turning
into the church garden—someone whispers
suddenly behind me on the ten-thousand-strong street.

A wagon from nowhere loaded
with seaweed! Maybe it's sending a message
from an unknown poem, maybe from a dead one's diary. Can you hear
this purely green, purely slimy, purely
corpse-heavy hope-sentence, too, my friends?
The summer can burn the back of our hands
in the sand, on the pitted stone table, on the
mountaintop, but our seeing and hearing eyes
may meet yet again in astonishment.

The Walnuts Tremble

I sit here again
in the motionless garden
and I don't expect eagles
instead of feathers anymore,
nor late resurrection.

What comes of its own will, will come,
what can come, will come:
in the morning the quick sun,
with axes flying high toward the forests,
at noon a suppressed sigh from the South,
which will make the belly
of outer space tremble.

And of course swallows come, too,
lonely,
they deftly fly between my fingers
held high,
as if they were flying into infinity
through the eye of the needle of the Strait of Gibraltar.

A miracle! A miracle!, I would have
exulted to myself in the past,
but now I just keep quiet,
knowing every apparition here
is an extension of my imagination.

Maybe the strong and unruly light is, too.
Maybe the trees.
I stand up, pat them
like the necks of good horses.
The walnuts tremble
as if each were
my green heart,

nuts which nothing, nothing,
not even Fate,
could individually judge.

Dialogue in the Mirror

Have you worn down? You sure have, and not just a little.
The tilting planes and tilting nooks
suit you even in the mirror. The towels
dangle like hanged swans.
Where, where are those epileptic, waltzing
fairies, the ones who so often danced past
your window with stutter-stepping hearts
while you fought night after night
with God? And where's the Adriatic Sea,
which showed you its beautiful teeth
at Duinó? It once was, now isn't.
Now it's like a reticent, married woman,
who'd dare smile at you only in her dreams.

Was it the bones that wore down? Or the flesh,
the era, the tendons? The unblindable snow
in your eyes? Or those countless, ray-spoked,
bronze desires which have kept, thus far,
your world taut? A razor's asleep on the shelf
next to your face: a knife with knees pulled to its chest.
It could be a child, or a bloodthirsty hostage.
Just don't wake it up! Just don't start talking
to it in the lamplight. Just stare at the white wall
behind it instead: the middle of the whitewash,
the whitewash. What's left of your endlessness
still whirls in it, as the morning light
whirls in a pupil strung tight.

Sulky Ode to the Pompeii Soldier

You little dumb Pompeii hero,
how many gods were you laid out next to
nobly, with a jaunty bunch
of Vesuvius' flowers on your chest? And how many
hollow-chested saints were shoved behind you in the line?
Consider this: your thin, rigid
little finger is more immortal than
my skull lugging one thousand brief days, brief nights,
and one thousand cemeteries! You're famous,
friend, although you died just once
on your guard post, unlike the others. And
even then in the pleasure of the universe. Orange-tree twigs,
palm leaves and rolling embers flowed around you
in the wedding march. Around me, though,
stinking war spit whirls in green, army excrement
and flute dirt again and again. To
escape from it? Where
and how? The mountain peaks and salt-white
heavenly bodies, too, are already infected.
At night I can see: the owls recruit mercenaries
to block the way there.

Elegy of Speed

Quickly,
quickly,
these days you have to write poems, too,
quickly, as the sun sets
at the mouth of the Garam River
and the shot-down plane is plunging,
tumbling toward the ground.
The wind,
the wind,
the full-bearded storm
sweeps panic-stricken
along the valley mistakenly left open,
above the Danube—who then
would find time to ponder twenty-four hours
about severed grasshopper legs,
lightning flashes,
when even death lights
seven candles all at once for a man?

If I ever had time—it's run out.
No more Rome, Prague,
no more New York launching
skyscraper-rockets,
only the adventure of my thinking of them
excites me again and again.
My head sometimes leans in
through twenty-thousand windows again.

I take a long look at a few
marble halls,
spiral stairs,
women's breasts accidentally left uncovered
and I quickly vanish from sight
like the paperboy, the morning thrushes.

Quickly,
quickly,
these days you have to write poems, too,
because what has been a poem till today
may not be a poem tomorrow,
only fleeting mercy,
only a quickly trickling drop of sweat.

Slow Down, Finally!

Even if everyone else is rushing about, don't you rush about!
Slow down, finally, before your death.
You find a shuddering tree everywhere,
    in which the forest stirs,
and a stone stamped with the prehistoric world's blemish.

You see: eyes are running toward the North
and toward the South. They leap from the shelves
of airplane hangars to swinging bells,
    then onto skyscrapers and the wreathes
of funeral processions walking to the sky,

as if they were chasing a snowflake lost
in their childhoods, as if a motherly kiss.
They are mad and hesitant. You can see in their every
    quiver that they no longer have a country,
just that hollowed eye-socket,

just that open space drawing inward,
where the world dies away in red, blue
and gray stains. Would you follow them?
    The eternally hungry and eternally
insatiable eyes? The martyrs

of uncertainty? Slow down, instead,
like the turtle who keeps peering from under its shell.
With the undulating rocking of your head
    centuries will begin to move in one rhythm. One century
of screams, the other of love.

And thus, step by step, all that you owned
can be yours again: ideas, devastation,
rumbling tunnels. And you'll have time, too,
    as you did in your teens,
to hug the resting mountains, the oxen chewing their cud.

Epilogue of the Dead Man

Thank you, gentlemen, for my quiet burial.
Thank you, thank you.
We did without the priest,
the bell-peal,
the rheumy sublimity.
We did without the scandal.

Though maybe the first degree murder
was a bit premature,
for the big toe on my foot would have gone,
even today, to God's party, but
it's no big deal: in this age
of noisy mass murders
the occasional hasty roadside slaughter
almost reassures.

It's uplifting, of course, that geniuses buried me:
full-templed and full-lived geniuses.
Behind them is every cathedral of Europe,
every library,
bile,
every breath
of the philosophers who chiseled
the diamonds and skies into such refinement.

Their words made the funeral parlor's roof tiles
sparkle,
and the crops of the pigeons ordered
to the wake swelled with pride to twice their size.
Wonderful, wonderful, I would have replied
to their parceled sentences, too,
for hadn't we been sliding
from the year of falcons
into the year of caterpillars—
but stuck to the ground

I could only think of hairy creatures
marching like accordions folding,
unfolding,
that would swarm the industrious leaves of the trees
and feast on them.

My apologies for this
coarse epilogue.
I'm not even muttering it to you,
gentlemen, but to myself.
If it weren't for these few tree-knots
and stones breaking my side, I'd be
silent as a grave. Along
with filleted pigs
and Wagner's mountable swan.

Slow, May Rain

It's raining, raining, just to rain.
For two hours my roof has been pattering.
The slender acacia clusters
    huddle together high above like girls
drenched to the skin at first communion.
The beautiful cache of their chastity can be seen.

Now and again a lightning flash hisses.
Madly, it runs to death.
My fits of jealously zigzagged
    through me like this, when
in my youth and stupidity I feared
to lose the world in every love.

Today I don't fear for anything
and I'm not afraid of anything. I've had
too many wars in my life, too many
    sleepless years and fragment-loves.
The trees of Budapest were wilting around me,
but I was breathing with the forest's lungs.

When I think of my past, how many rains like this
keep falling! How many tiny chainlinks
from the fingers of God! And they're not
    just pattering on my roof, but also on my bones.
On the bright foreheads of my dead which,
like stopped clocks, watch and call me to account.

It's raining, raining, just to rain.
For two hours my roof has been pattering.
The slender acacia clusters
    huddle together high above like girls
drenched to the skin at first communion.
The beautiful cache of their chastity can be seen.

Again the Sugarless, Bitter Tea

Again this taste of sugarless,
bitter tea in my mouth. Again this taste of shame.
Have I failed once more? Or have I just lost?
Swallows soar
in through my open window
as though offering condolences
silently, without witnesses.

I should strike them down, too,
with a straight-arm, like the multitudes
of riffraff gloating on the street.
They just hang around the boulevards
with sauntering hips, licking ice cream
and impertinently snickering
into my eyes from among the shadows.

Many little, powdered skulls!

If they were born five times to this world
they still wouldn't understand what grieves me—
they lack five hearts,
five brains,
and fifty thousand memories from the past.

Five beheaded peonies
lie on Vérmzó.
Not one of the gloaters knows
I can't help but think of my mother country
knocked on her back
when I see those five peonies lined up in a row.

Never mind! Let them dance, sniggering,
in front of me, their right hands holding
trained falcons or ice cream.

Let them have a few summers again.
Let them have them with the airy poppies
and the planets lit like advertisements.

Bitter, Pre-Whitsun Song

If they ousted me,
    well, they ousted me;
no dented iron bucket or shirt-skirted
muse will cry for me.
I look at the sky again as
    my own, tried partner.

Whitsun is coming, beautiful, rumpled holiday.
    Those who defeated me
are walking up the hills one after the other,
expecting the swishing, fiery tongues
of flame above their heads:
    the holy spirit-orchids.

They're expecting
    glory
after the power. Let it be. Let it be.
The heart echoes it in me:
this alarm-raising, rocky wall of Tihany.
    Since I don't need

anything that's not my own
    miracle anymore.
I smile at the grass that grew
from beneath the dead stone, the way
happy conspirators exchange glances,
    and the smile turns me into

the person who tumbled from a star
    a long time ago,
through the clouds, through
the undulating, dark tapestry of birds
and touched earth like rain,
    like a bit of sun that also shines at night.

Ousted, I keep walking, loitering around you.
    Exiled
in my country, only on this green promenade
of God can I hear the crickets begin to sing
encouragingly. They sing for me the psalms
    of Whitsun from

the trampled grass. Almost from under the ground:
    from the country
of Eternal Ashes. They sing in the language
of the dead instead of fiery tongues.
Can you hear what swarming is arising,
    what grumblings are growing strong?

Elegy of the Eyes Left Without Makeup

Letter to Andrew Morton, English Poet

I've never seen you, don't know who you are.
The employee of what kind of dreams and what
kind of citizen? Burly? Tall and lean? A wandering,
fine fog-man from England? The friend of horses,
dogs? Or of the gulls moored
in the scalloped bay? I just read a few
of your poems tonight in a brand new,
creaking book. Snow, snow everywhere,
where you step, where you look, where
God drops a handkerchief on the ground.
Maybe you invented the snow-white nightfall
around Essex, you who for years have made
pilgrimages to a hospital bed. Nowhere is there
any kind of longitudinal mourning line in the countryside
of your land, England. Nowhere a leafless,
black tree, a black post, a black forest.
Nowhere a black flock of birds bearing
an easy coffin. Tell me
who that mysterious living-dead woman in white
is there on the bed? That eternally snow-covered,
breathing body? Your mother? Girlfriend? Wife?
The Ophelia of Paradise undermined from without?
It seems I knew that breathing woman
from someplace. The wounds sliced with knives
on her head and chest, the abyss of oblivion in her eyes.
Her black hair, fallen out, tosses even today
in the gas-vapor commotion of the streets,
gets coiled on the streetcars' axelrods,
hisses, weeps, turns then springs
up above the shoulders hurrying to work,
and then to me, up here, to the tremulous room
where her eye-makeup kit
lies like an extinct volcano or dried-up lake.
Later, when we meet again,
I'll also tell you, in snowfall, the story

of the eyes left without makeup,
and of the hospital candles snuffed out early.

End-of-Summer Exhaustion

I've grown exhausted as the plundered
earth grows exhausted by the end of summer.
My swishing juices have rolled, drop by drop, asunder,
have evaporated and, now and then, a stray bird
thanks me for letting it drink from them.

I look at my resting, weather-beaten fists
propped here on the fence post. Graves? Clods?
I'm more likely to see my father's tired face in them.
He'd stare straight ahead after stacking like this,
half-dead, the parched sky and dry lightning behind him.

Oh, these knotty peasant faces, fists,
idols, so distant from the soft violets,
so far from the plentiful waters! As if
axe-hewn memories were gathering around me—
always in summer—and those men of vanished gods,

who migrated, needy, straight from the sun
here to the earth so they might scythe,
break stubble. They disappeared, died
long ago, but I still grow tired with them
in the stifling cornfields, the meadows filled with anthills,

where the scythe slices the necks of bloated,
little cows, and also slices the rainbow.
I'm standing in the sun, I keep stiffening
and withering. Nearby I hear the hollow moan
of a struck tree. This, too, is music!

Music, music, tree-hymn, that only the bones
banished above the earth can truly hear.

Not Even Poets

There are as many poems as people
on a promenade. They come, push, shove
and press my heart to the wall now and then.
Some are like a young, clean-shaven
nun's head: the summer glows
around it, the lost world's stifling sensuality,
the nakedness of groins, thighs, and abdomens.
Another is like a sleepwalking skeleton,
but it arrives from the South with a parasol,
brass rattles and pruned baby hands on its ankles.
Old Venice's dancer of death? Or
war-plagued Bosnia's? Trench mortars,
bells, cannons, the crackling of clappers big
as a windmill sail, accompany his dance. But who
will stop to shudder on the squares, at the foot-
statues startled awake by such a clamor?
Who will set fire to their living hair
so dread and love might stand
on their feet together?

Everything I Had

Everything I had, I gave to others:
my time, my patience, the cloudless
afternoons of my wasps. The stripped
winter forest, which looked like a gigantic
hedgehog from a distance. And the money, the money,
the pathetic money, like somebody
dispensing gold with St. László's hand.

Many laughed at me, too, like a daft
monk. They laughed but they followed
me in a large crew. They came
morning and night; they came
blackened from among the tossed-aside railroad ties,
from the colorful throng of city neon-butterflies,
they came from the timeless time of sunbathing books,
clotted scarves or faded handkerchiefs on their necks.

I wasn't their savior. I was their fool.
A promising, independent thief who
loathes alcohol, blood, nursing nicotine,
but one day may have an honored place
on Golgotha—and a sty, a dead-end street,
a species of smile growing extinct
can be named after him at the millennium's end,
if there's anyone left to do such things.

Only barbaric hopes and miracle-expecting hours
are ticking around me, like the undamaged clock
of the car that crashed into a tree. But where, now,
shall I look for a clearly visible God,
a true fool, laughable, to take my place,
one who would squanderingly hand out his hands, his voice,
his imagination, the big mountains sprawling within him again,
who might even be pleased now and then since
the looted November sky resembles his looted face?

Is Anything Left?

Do I still have a chance?
A tough game, an adult hide-and-seek
or a masked ball near the morgue?
The sun shines in my face; outside the abandoned shepherd's hut
twenty-seven butterflies are drying themselves.

Is there still a miracle left
in me trying to prove itself
so I, too, might soar
with butterflies and dust?

I've grown heavy from winter's chandelier indifference
of room nooks and meeting rooms.
The chairs, like bribed witnesses, stood round me—

Is there still a protecting,
womanly smile, womanly prophecy,
so someday even my second descent into hell
might end: the dance of lice on the back of my neck, end?

Sometimes I feel: it was better for me to be
hopeless but strong in the forty-year camp
than to be the master now of fouled hope.
I go to sleep and wake each morning with bleeding words,
with neurotic violets, like refugees
from the South, who left everything
only to find themselves at the foot of a shoddy wall.

From grass to bush, from clod to cracked rock,
I run my eyes: where does
the final sign flash that makes even prodigal sons
turn back? Perhaps in the eyes of a thrush?
In a woman's scarf flapping into the sky?
Perhaps in the sleepwalking, cemetery dust
which, like a whirlwind, also appears at bright noon?

The Newspaper's Rustling

The newspaper's rustling, they're reviling me again.
Hired, big spitters take aim at me bravely
for their own sakes. It's either the fury of mating
or the frenzy of funeral feasts broken out in them:
they're shouting with joy that the snake put to sleep
was hidden by me in the ruined flower bouquet,
and by me, me, in the bowl of strawberries.

Today I'm just a plain plotter
in their eyes, a leader sleeping with icicles,
the planner of wars, with swans in cannon fire,
but even tomorrow, like a rambling thief,
I'll steal as well: money, bells, holy statues,
macaroni and a foal galloping in the sky,
because my hands can reach even that far.

Go on, you nobodies with your wild imaginings,
out with my crimes. Let me know at last
what's lying hidden deep inside me: what outrages,
like Villon's, are there beneath the quilted modesty!
But beware: the mixing of trashy blood
and trashy gold soon grows boring
in the pestilent news, and only women will be left
as stimulants, the women: buttocks pressed
against the wall, breasts sprinkled with Martini.

Or did they, too, grow extinct in you long ago,
like Hortobágy's Russian oaks—
extinct—even in your dreams?
Don't you ever learn, my reviling benefactors,
what kind of paradise I spend every night in
these days to save myself from you,
watching for a long time from down here
as light glimmers through the tops of the poplars.

Soul and Water

Rhymes have left me
like the girls who gaze
even at each other.
Left me, like unforeseen, clandestine
lovemakings in borrowed,
paradisical rooms.
I just write one line after another irritably
as if I were drinking very strong, undomesticated coffee.
One line after another,
without echoing bell-peals.
Even Babylonian psalms used
to rhyme for me in the past:
they coupled like the cast off,
wingless stone and bull-brow.
Today only the swishing
closed glass elevators
of convention centers
watch each other with suspicion from afar
as if they had nothing to do with what they saw.
And in the air, too, big, eyeballs stand out,
roll lonely
and lost, long eyelashes
like black, mourning veils from Sarajevo.
Who can, who dares stand shamelessly
outside his blistering door
to wait with pounding heart
for a walnut leaf to fall in his face,
who can, who dares rest by big waters,
like the old, nomadic tribes,
so soul and water might answer each other?

Questions, to You

Tell me: is there a whole day,
morning and night, in which the sedge
leaf also sharpens,
and your shout, racing on water, reaches
the other side? Is there a blade of grass
from whose tip a drop of dew falls on your lap?

It's summer; the apples are ripening in the garden,
and the lettering on the cemetery's new, artificial
marble stone is fading. Tell me: are there human eyes
that blast off every day
like rockets to the moon, taking with them
the color of apples and of gold,
to blend them together before going to sleep?
Or are there only fragmentary, fallen-to-pieces
worlds throbbing everywhere? Dust here?
Bee legs stuck in resin over there?
And volcanoes like prematurely
buried hearts in the mountain depths?
And cities upon cities with rapidly
pulsating veins and with stomachs
sunk under the earth? Tell me: who's
crying alone in the forest even now,
trying to find his God
before night falls?

Denunciation

You've always been more solemn
    than you should have been.
You even heard an organ playing there,
    where only darkness,
        or a shattered oak forest,
    grew more and more dense.
Legions of splinters pressed into your heart:
the gaunt advance guard of daggers and knives,
    but you just waved it away:
you'll worry when the army arrives,
    when the commandos in black
        headdress arrive.

Know this—he who loved you well would have loved you
    even if you'd condemned them all,
        or had broken bones
on the day of wrath and at the festival of apples left out to rot,
if you'd dared to throw stones
at the violets prying into your affairs.

It's still not too late!
You can have a last life—not just a last word!
A last card trick! Restrained tornados throb
behind every one of your words—
with swarming ladybirds grown gray
and weapons awakening along with your body.
Do you dare, this final time, to be hopeless
like a grinning beast, or God?

Late October Night

The night's cold, beautiful.
The groundskeeper's torching
the cleared, dry cornfield.
And the flames slowly set out
for the Danube
as when you left
for the ball in your full-length, yellow dress.

There are no violins here, no drums, no clarinets.
Just some voice swishes, grates
above me in the night,
as if your heavy hair
that I've inherited
were now being dragged behind the clouds
by ethereal wild geese.

The deer, too, stop
to listen to the rustle.
And indeed, it is you
who marches across their dilated pupils.
You're walking out of the hospital for good,
in disguise, leaving death
instead of yourself on the bed.

There's no lake in front of you, no stone,
no storm, no frightening quince-apple hill
on the road winding toward the graveyard.
You can amble freely between the poplars,
while, between unlit candles,
the chicory-eyed, crazed woman—
even as she approaches—is moving away.

The night's cold, beautiful.
Late October night, crystalline, blue.
The eyes of the pheasants, frightened

by the cornstalk fires, gleam
yellow from the top of the hill.
Shivering, I retreat beneath
the remaining yellow-gleaming walnut leaves.

To Sleep, to Sleep

To sleep, to sleep, it doesn't matter where:
on the church step, in a ditch, on a beach, in the weeds
with great big burdock leaves on my face
or with the sky sinking deeply down.

The summer could rattle beside my ear
like horse-hide hung out to dry,
the well chain and train could clatter,
as well as every soup kitchen iron pot and plate,

and meanwhile I'd keep sinking
into that deep water, that quiet senselessness,
where noiseless doors and tossed-off shirts are swinging,
the woolen scarves of my dead. And no one

would ask: where are you from, where are you going? No one
ask why I've been walking around with clenched teeth
among the miserable little conquerors for years
like a lumberjack in the cemetery? No one,

no one ask whether my life now is a life
or a prison? Pear tree leaves, pears
and daisies would fall, drop above me,
a dropped ring, a dropped hand and a scrap of sack,

like clods of earth on a corpse. Rippling
sand might be my bed, or tortuous
gravel. And the blood branches, too,
would be long sleeping, gently, in my closed eyes.

Scarecrows on the Hill

Incomplete Sonnet

Who knows why, but I've really been waiting
for this day. On the hilltop, up there,
two scarecrows suddenly appeared in the summer.
King and queen. I knew right away

they wanted to pay their respects to me, only
to me, with their tattered elegance. In the skirted
lady's hand, a half-eaten melon rind. In the seedy
lord's hand, a broken Coke bottle instead

of a scepter. All around them, butterflies flitted:
the excited people of the court. And the light
above them was the light of ten thousand coins.

Or was it perhaps the available-on-order smile
of the republic? Nothing's down-payment?
The idiotic halo of a stagnant era that's tempted me so often?

Still Life in Our Pantry at Home

I've been leaning against the wall here for hours
and the flour bag's been leaning over there.
Oh, this purblind pantry
could be my prison too!
A smoke-reeking rod looms black
above my head: the forsaken space of sausages, hams.
And what a window is watching me! A robust
eagle could soar through it
only with its wings cut off.

So this is the home I longed to return to from gnashing
cities,
from the demonstrations of litter
flying high above the streets?
I longed to return here to the mouse-pissed hole,
me, the heir of whitewashed walls and smothering rye smell?
True: I first saw the stars rise
on evening bridles here,
the moon,
and the First World War bayonet hung
threateningly above me here,
like the sword of blackmailing, little gods.

I learned, later, to shudder
and not fear in this decaying nook,
where the waylaying lightning flashes would drop in.
A dead soldier lay here,
as well as a machine-gunned pig
with a medal-of-honor wound in its throat.
A shriveled brother-in-law grown
lonely lay here, too,
left a widower by the war.

If I could, I'd move away from the wall,
away, with my body's full weight,
but some part of my past holds me here,
defiant temple-light and seeping mother's weeping.
And I love this place consecrated with blood,
this lonely, peasant place of prophecy,
where a wrinkle-faced white angel might step out
of the stuffy flour bag—
We'd stare for a long, long time at each other,
like bats stiffened in amber.

Ringing in the Ear

My ears are ringing, ringing, like
poor Arany's ears, from morning to night.
Maybe it's distant grindstones and pig-killing
knives that are continuously whimpering?
Or is it just crickets walled up in my body
crying in their falsetto voice? For whom?
Why? For me? Themselves?

But why couldn't this suspended
eternal note in me be
that of ballads and countries
flayed alive?
How many times have I stood by
the bloody scene, in the heap
of ruins and corpses, when it was possible
only to whimper silently, inside.

Do you now and then hear such a clamor
in yourselves, my sonnet and key-ring
rattling friends? There's peace in trees,
I know; the scales scraped off fish
fall dully into the sand, but up,
high above, it's as if hearts, hands and heads
of hair crammed into ice trains swished.

My ears are ringing, ringing, like
poor Arany's. I can see his averted face,
he's waiting for the silence. But there's no more
lonely, earthly silence. There's no more
lonely screaming either. The air is blustering
and howling there in the leaves of the mulberry tree,
there, there, the beyond-death music is playing.

ACKNOWLEDGMENTS

Grateful acknowledgment is made to to publications where the following translations appeared:

Agni: "Biographical Fragment";
American Literary Review: "Questions, to You";
The American Poetry Review: "Wandering in a Former Party Office Building," "Ringing in the Ear," "I Don't Deny It: My Eyes Are Darker," "Dialogue in the Mirror";
ACM (Another Chicago Magazine): "February Vision," "To Sleep, to Sleep," "I Look Back and Don't See Myself";
Artful Dodge: "Where Are My Betters Who Fell Behind?," "Everything I Had," "Late Winter Morning," "Because There Was a Time";
Boulevard: "I Was Watching the Bushes," "Poets, My Fellows";
Chelsea: "You Look at Me Like," "Courtyard at Home, Before the War," "Poem, to Diogenes," "August Evening," "If You Were God's Relative";
Denver Quarterly: "Scarecrows on the Hill," "Injured Poem";
Field: "Etching of a Small Town," "Widows Danced," "Remembering November, 1956," "I, Too, Might Have Been," "Epilogue of the Dead Man," "Returning Home from Flight After the War";
Grand Street: "So You Won't Be a Witness Today, Either";
Indiana Review: "I Wanted to Arrange";
International Poetry Review: "Elegy of the Eyes Left Without Makeup," "Sulky Ode to the Pompeii Soldier," "Farewell to Finland";
Kenyon Review: "Morning Awakening," "If I Had Believed";
The Literary Review: "Metamorphosis in Stockholm," "Can You Still Hear It?," "Among the Ferns of Finland," "Autumn";
Luna: "Again the Sugarless, Bitter Tea," "Slow Down, Finally!," "Bitter, Pre-Whitsun Song," "I Rip a Blade of Grass in Half";
Mark: "The Nook Was Fine for Me";
The Massachusetts Review: "Sunday Still Life—with Table, with Knife";
Mid-American Review (chapbook): "End-of-Summer Exhaustion," "If This Were Life," "Soul and Water," "Sometimes I Watch Her," "January Apparition," "The Newspaper's Rustling," "Is Anything Left?," "Metamorphosis in Stockholm," "Elegy of the Eyes Left Without

Makeup," "Young Nuns of Rome," "I Should Go Blind," "In the
    Summer, I Can Hear a Clatter of Hooves," "You Look at Me Like";
New England Review: "The Citizen of the Garden," "Not Even Poets";
New Letters: "You Are Free, Almost Guiltily Free," "Slow, May Rain";
Northwest Review: "Seasons at Odds with Themselves," "February Vision,"
    "Godless Summer," "Late October Night," "Fleeing Soldier, 1944,"
    "Diary, Early Fall of 1982," "There Are Only Days," "Holy and
    Wicked Time";
Partisan Review: "In Filtered Shade," "May the Water Keep Vigil with
    Me";
Poetry East: "The Time Has Come";
Poetry International: "Flying Above Thirty Thousand Feet";
Poet Lore: "Bicycle Racers," "I Can See Their Eyes";
The Seneca Review: "I'll Bear Your Slow Purification";
Southern Review: "The Day After Easter";
Translation: "My Masters";
Willow Springs: "Monuments of the World."

"My Masters," "A Night Journey into Germany," and "The Nook Was Fine
for Me" were published in *Selected Poems of Sándor Csoóri*, Copper Canyon
Press, 1992.

These following translations have also appeared in various anthologies
and selections:

Anthology of Magazine Verse & Yearbook of American Poetry: "May the
    Water Keep Vigil with Me," "Can You Still Hear It?";
The World's Best Poetry: "Wandering in a Former Party Office Building";
The Vintage Book of Contemporary World Poetry: "My Masters."

My thanks to Anette Marta, László Vertes, and, especially, Mária Szende
who created the literal drafts of many of these poems. I would never have
been able to create these versions without them. I am also grateful to the
Fulbright Commission, the Witter Bynner Foundation, the Soros Founda-
tion and the National Endowment for the Humanities for awards that
allowed me the time to work on these translations.

ABOUT THE AUTHOR

Sándor Csoóri, one of Hungary's most prominent and outspoken poets, is the author of sixteen books of poetry, six books of essays, two novels, and several film scripts. His poetry spans five decades, with his first book, *The Bird Takes Wing*, published in 1954 and his most recent book, *Quiet Vertigo*, appearing in 2001. In addition to being one of Hungary's most widely-read writers, his work has been translated into every major European language, as well as Japanese and Chinese.

Csoóri also has received numerous awards for his poetry, including the Attila József Prize in Poetry, The Hungarian Book of the Year Award (1995), the Károli Gáspár Award, the Hungarian Heritage Award and the prestigious Kossuth Award, Hungary's greatest honor for achievement in artistic or scientific work. He was a major figure in the founding of the Hungarian Democratic Forum and was Chairman of the World Federation of Hungarians from 1991–2000. He is a leading proponent for the rights of ethnic Hungarians in other countries.

ABOUT THE TRANSLATOR

Len Roberts is the translator of two chapbooks and one previous full-length volume of Sándor Csoóri's poetry, as well as the author of eight books of his own poetry. *The Silent Singer: New and Selected Poems* (University of Illinois Press, 2001) is his most recent book. He has received a fellowship from the John Simon Guggenheim Foundation, two grants from the National Endowment for the Arts, and a grant from the National Endowment for the Humanities for his translation work. His fourth book of poems, *Black Wings*, was selected for the National Poetry Series. His poems and translations have appeared in the *American Poetry Review*, *Poetry*, *Paris Review*, and *Partisan Review*, among others, and in anthologies such as the *Vintage Book of Contemporary World Poetry* and *In Quest of the Miracle Stag*.

The Lannan Translations Selection Series

Ljuba Merlina Bortolani, *The Siege*

Olga Orozco, *Engravings Torn from Insomnia*

Gérard Martin, *The Hiddenness of the World*

Fadhil Al-Azzawi, *Miracle Maker*

Sándor Csoóri, *Before and After the Fall*

For more on the Lannan Translations Selection Series
visit our Web site:
www. boaeditions.org